Little Bible Heroes™
Heroes of Babylon

Written by Victoria Kovacs
Illustrated by David Ryley

B&H KIDS
NASHVILLE, TENNESSEE

GOLDQUILL
WWW.GOLDQUILL.CO.UK

Published by B&H Publishing Group 2016. Text and illustrations copyright © 2016, GoldQuill, United Kingdom.
All rights reserved. Scripture quotations are taken from the Holman Christian Standard Bible ® Copyright © 1999,
2000, 2002, 2003, 2009 by Holman Bible Publishers. Used by permission.
ISBN: 978-1-4336-4325-5   Dewey Decimal Classification: CE
Subject Heading: HEROES OF BABYLON \ RUTH \ BIBLE STORIES
Printed in June 2017 in Heshan, Guangdong, China
3 4 5 6 7 8 • 21 20 19 18 17

Shadrach, Meshach, and Abednego are three Hebrews who serve the king of Babylon.

One day, the king makes a golden statue. He commands everyone to bow down and worship it.

Shadrach, Meshach, and Abednego know it is wrong to bow down to an idol. "We will not serve your gods or worship the golden statue," they tell the king.

The king is furious. He orders his guards to throw Shadrach, Meshach, and Abednego into a fiery furnace to punish them.

Suddenly, the king is startled. He sees a fourth man in the furnace with the three friends. They are saved!

The three men walk out of the flames. Not one hair on their heads is singed! They don't even smell like smoke!

The king says, "Praise to the God of Shadrach, Meshach, and Abednego. No other god can save like He can!"

Read:

Nebuchadnezzar exclaimed, "Praise to the God of Shadrach, Meshach, and Abednego! He sent His angel and rescued His servants who trusted in Him."—Daniel 3:28

Think:

1. Who did the king see in the fire with Shadrach, Meshach, and Abednego?
2. Can you think of a time you said no to doing something you knew was wrong?

Remember:

God wants us to always do what we know is right.

Read:
May the Lord reward you for what you have done, and may you receive a full reward from the Lord God of Israel, under whose wings you have come for refuge.—Ruth 2:12

Think:
1. What did Ruth tell Naomi she would do?
2. Ruth collected grain to take care of her family. What are some things you can do for your family?

Remember:
God wants us to help others.

God blesses Ruth and Boaz
with a baby boy. His name
is Obed, and he is one of the
ancestors of Jesus!

Boaz marries Ruth. He knows she is kind and good.

Ruth works all through the harvests to provide for her mother-in-law.

Boaz owns the fields. He sees Ruth and hears how she helps Naomi. He tells his workers to leave her extra grain so that she and Naomi will have enough.

In Bethlehem, Ruth goes into the fields to gather leftover stalks of grain so she and Naomi will have food to eat.

Her mother-in-law, Naomi, decides to return to her hometown of Bethlehem. Ruth tells her, "Wherever you go, I will go. Your God will be my God."

Ruth lives in the land of Moab. Sadly, her husband and his brother and father all die.

Little Bible Heroes™

Ruth

Written by Victoria Kovacs
Illustrated by David Ryley

B&H KIDS
NASHVILLE, TENNESSEE

GOLDQUILL
WWW.GOLDQUILL.CO.UK

Published by B&H Publishing Group 2016. Text and illustrations copyright © 2016, GoldQuill, United Kingdom.
All rights reserved. Scripture quotations are taken from the Holman Christian Standard Bible ® Copyright © 1999,
2000, 2002, 2003, 2009 by Holman Bible Publishers. Used by permission.
ISBN: 978-1-4336-4325-5   Dewey Decimal Classification: CE
Subject Heading: HEROES OF BABYLON \ RUTH \ BIBLE STORIES
Printed in June 2017 in Heshan, Guangdong, China
3 4 5 6 7 8 • 21 20 19 18 17